INTRODUCTION

V/. We adore you, O Christ, and we bless you.

R/. **Because by your holy Cross you have redeemed the world.**

Meditation

When the Apostle Philip asked Jesus, "Master, show us the Father," he replied, "Have I been with you for so long a time and you still do not know me, Philip? Whoever has seen me has seen the Father" (Jn 14:8-9). This evening, as we accompany Jesus in our hearts while he makes his way beneath the Cross, let us not forget those words. Even as he carries the Cross, even in his Death on the Cross, Jesus remains the Son, who is one with God the Father. When we look upon his face disfigured by beating, weariness, and inner suffering, we see the face of the Father. Indeed, it is precisely in this moment that God's glory, his surpassing splendor, in some way becomes visible on the face of Jesus. In this poor, suffering man whom Pilate, in the hope of eliciting compassion, showed to the Jews with the words "Behold, the man!" (Jn 19:5), we see revealed the true greatness of God, that mysterious grandeur beyond all our imagining.

Yet in the crucified Jesus we see revealed another kind of grandeur: our own greatness, the grandeur which belongs to every man and woman by the simple fact that we have a human face and heart. In the words of St. Anthony of Padua, "Christ, who is your life, hangs before you, so that you can gaze upon the Cross as if in a mirror . . . If you look upon him, you will be able to see the greatness of your dignity and worth . . . Nowhere else can we better recognize our own value, than by looking into the mirror of the Cross" (*Sermones dominicales et festivi*, III, pp. 213-214). Jesus, the Son of God, died for you, for me, for each of us. In this way he gave us concrete proof of how great and precious we are in the eyes of God, the only eyes capable of seeing beyond all appearances and of peering into the depths of our being.

As we make the *Way of the Cross*, let us ask God to grant us this gaze of truth and love, so that, in union with him, we may become free and good.

The Holy Father:

In the name of the Father, and of the Son, and of the Holy Spirit.

R/. Amen.

The Holy Father:

Let us pray.

A moment of silence follows.

Lord God, almighty Father,
you know all things
and you see, hidden within our hearts, our great need for you.
Grant each of us the humility to acknowledge this need.
Free our mind from the pretension,
wrong-headed and even ridiculous,

OFFICE FOR THE LITURGICAL CELEBRATIONS
OF THE SUPREME PONTIFF

THE WAY
OF THE CROSS
AT THE COLOSSEUM

LED BY THE HOLY FATHER
BENEDICT XVI

GOOD FRIDAY 2010

Meditations and prayers by His Eminence Cardinal Camillo Ruini, Vicar General Emeritus of His Holiness for the Diocese of Rome.

Cover Photo by CNS/Paul Haring

First printing, January 2011
Second printing, March 2011

ISBN 978-1-60137-148-5

that we can master the mystery which embraces us.
Free our will from the presumption,
equally naïve and unfounded,
that we can create our own happiness
and the meaning of our lives.
Enlighten and purify our inner eye,
and enable us to recognize, free of all hypocrisy,
the evil which lies within us.
But grant us too,
in the light of the Cross and Resurrection of your only Son,
the certainty that, united to him and sustained by him,
we too can overcome evil with good.
Lord Jesus,
help us, in this spirit, to walk behind your Cross.

R/. Amen.

Jesus is condemned to death

V/. We adore you, O Christ, and we bless you.

R/. Because by your holy Cross you have redeemed the world.

From the Gospel according to John   19:6-7, 12, 16

When the chief priests and the guards saw him they cried out, "Crucify him, crucify him!" Pilate said to them, "Take him yourselves and crucify him. I find no guilt in him." The Jews answered, "We have a law, and according to that law he ought to die, because he made himself the Son of God."...

Consequently, Pilate tried to release him; but the Jews cried out, "If you release him, you are not a Friend of Caesar. Everyone who makes himself a king opposes Caesar."...

Then he handed him over to them to be crucified.

Meditation

Why was Jesus, the one who "went about doing good" (Acts 10:38), condemned to death? This question will accompany us along the Way of the Cross, even as it accompanies us throughout our lives.

In the Gospels we find a true answer: the Jewish leaders wanted his death, because they understood that Jesus considered himself the Son of God. We also find an answer that the Jews used as a pretext, in order to obtain his condemnation from Pilate: Jesus pretended to be a king of this world, the king of the Jews.

But behind this answer there opens up an abyss, to which the Gospels and indeed all of Sacred Scripture direct our gaze: Jesus died for our sins. And on an even deeper level, he died for us, he died because God loves us, and he loves us even to giving us his only Son, that we might have life through him (cf. Jn 3:16-17).

It is to ourselves, then, that we must look: to the evil and the sin that dwell within us and that all too often we pretend to ignore. Yet all the more should we turn our eyes to the God who is rich in mercy and who has called us his friends (cf. Jn 15:15). Thus the Way of the Cross and the entire journey of our life become a way of penance, pain, and conversion, but also of gratitude, faith, and joy.

All:

Our Father, who art in heaven,
hallowed be thy name.
Thy kingdom come.
Thy will be done on earth, as it is in heaven.
Give us this day our daily bread;
and forgive us our trespasses
as we forgive those who trespass against us,
and lead us not into temptation,
but deliver us from evil. Amen.

At the Cross her station keeping,
Stood the mournful Mother weeping,
Close to Jesus to the last.

JESUS CARRIES HIS CROSS

V/. We adore you, O Christ, and we bless you.

R/. Because by your holy Cross you have redeemed the world.

From the Gospel according to Matthew   27:27-31

Then the soldiers of the governor took Jesus inside the praetorium and gathered the whole cohort around him. They stripped off his clothes and threw a scarlet military cloak about him. Weaving a crown out of thorns, they placed it on his head, and a reed in his right hand. And kneeling before him, they mocked him, saying, "Hail, King of the Jews!" They spat upon him and took the reed and kept striking him on the head. And when they had mocked him, they stripped him of the cloak, dressed him in his own clothes, and led him off to crucify him.

From the Gospel according to John   19:17

Carrying the Cross himself he went out to what is called the Place of the Skull, in Hebrew, Golgotha.

Condemnation is followed by humiliation. What the soldiers do to Jesus seems inhuman to us. Indeed, it is inhuman: these are acts of mockery and contempt that express a dark savagery, indifferent to the suffering, including physical suffering, needlessly inflicted upon someone already condemned to the ghastly torture of the Cross. And yet the behavior of the soldiers is also, sadly, all too human. A thousand pages from the books of the history of humanity and the daily news confirm that actions of this kind are not at all foreign to man. The Apostle Paul has clearly expressed this paradox: "I know that good does not dwell in me, that is, in my flesh. . . . For I do not do the good I want, but the evil I do not want" (Rom 7:18-19).

And so it is: in our conscience shines the light of goodness, a light which in many cases is bright and guides us, fortunately, in our decisions. But often the opposite occurs: this light becomes obscured by resentment, by unspeakable cravings, by the perversion of our heart. And then we become cruel, capable of the worst, even of things unbelievable.

Lord Jesus, I am one of those who reviled and struck you. It was you yourself who said, "Whatever you did for one of these least brothers of mine, you did for me" (Mt 25:40). Lord Jesus, forgive me.

All:

Our Father . . .

Through her heart, his sorrow sharing,
All his bitter anguish bearing,
Now at length the sword had passed.

THIRD STATION

Jesus falls the first time

V/. We adore you, O Christ, and we bless you.

R/. Because by your holy Cross you have redeemed the world.

From the Book of the Prophet Isaiah   53:4-6

Yet it was our infirmities that he bore,
*   our sufferings that he endured,*
While we thought of him as stricken,
*   as one smitten by God and afflicted.*
But he was pierced for our offenses,
*   crushed for our sins,*
Upon him was the chastisement that makes us whole,
*   by his stripes we were healed.*
We had all gone astray like sheep,
*   each following his own way;*
But the LORD laid upon him
*   the guilt of us all.*

MEDITATION

The Gospels do not record Jesus falling beneath the Cross, yet this ancient tradition is very likely. We have only to remember that, before taking up his Cross, Jesus had been flogged at Pilate's command. After all that had happened after nightfall in the Garden of Olives, his strength would have been, for all intents and purposes, spent.

Before turning our attention to the most profound and interior aspects of Jesus' Passion, let us take a moment to consider the physical pain that he was forced to endure. Enormous, awful pain, even to his last breath on the Cross, a pain which had to be frightful.

Physical suffering is the easiest type of pain to eliminate, or at least to ease, with our modern techniques and practices, with anesthetics or other pain treatments. Even though, for many reasons, whether natural or due to human behavior, a massive amount of physical suffering continues to be present in the world.

In any event, Jesus did not refuse physical suffering, and thus he entered into solidarity with the whole human family, especially all the many people whose lives, even today, are filled with this kind of pain. As we watch him fall beneath his Cross, let us humbly ask him for the courage to break open, in a solidarity which goes beyond mere words, the narrowness of our hearts.

All:

Our Father ...

Oh, how sad and sore distressed
Was that Mother highly blessed
Of the sole begotten One!

Jesus meets his Mother

V/. We adore you, O Christ, and we bless you.

R/. Because by your holy Cross you have redeemed the world.

From the Gospel according to John   19:25-27

Standing by the Cross of Jesus were his mother and his mother's sister, Mary the wife of Clopas, and Mary of Magdala. When Jesus saw his mother and the disciple there whom he loved, he said to his mother, "Woman, behold, your son." Then he said to the disciple, "Behold, your mother." And from that hour the disciple took her into his home.

MEDITATION

The Gospels do not directly recount a meeting between Jesus and his Mother along the Way of the Cross, but speak instead of the presence of Mary standing at the foot of the Cross. There Jesus speaks to her and to the beloved disciple, the Evangelist John. His words have an immediate meaning: he entrusts Mary to John, so that he might take care of her. Yet his words also have a broader and more profound meaning: at the foot of the Cross Mary is called to utter a second "yes," after the "yes" which she spoke at the Annunciation, when she became the Mother of Jesus and thus opened the door to our salvation.

With this second "yes," Mary becomes the Mother of us all, the Mother of every man and woman for whom Jesus shed his blood. Here motherhood is a living sign of God's love and mercy for us. Because of this, the bonds of affection and trust uniting the Christian people to Mary are deep and strong. As a result, we have recourse to her spontaneously, especially at the most difficult times of our lives.

Mary, however, paid a high price for this universal motherhood. Simeon had prophesied of her in the Temple of Jerusalem: "And you yourself a sword will pierce" (Lk 2:35).

Mary, Mother of Jesus and our Mother, help us to feel in our hearts, tonight and always, the love-filled suffering which joined you to the Cross of your Son.

All:

Our Father . . .

Christ above in torment hangs,
She beneath beholds the pangs
Of her dying, glorious Son.

Simon of Cyrene helps Jesus carry his Cross

V/. We adore you, O Christ, and we bless you.

R/. **Because by your holy Cross you have redeemed the world.**

From the Gospel according to Luke   23:26

As they led him away they took hold of a certain Simon, a Cyrenian, who was coming in from the country; and after laying the Cross on him, they made him carry it behind Jesus.

Meditation

Jesus must have been completely exhausted, and so the soldiers took the first unlucky person they could find and told him to carry the Cross. So too, in everyday life, the cross, in many different forms—whether as sickness or a serious accident, the death of a loved one or the loss of work—falls upon us, often unexpectedly. We see in this only a stroke of bad luck, or at worst, a tragedy.

Jesus, however, said to his disciples, "Whoever wishes to come after me must deny himself, take up his cross, and follow me" (Mt 16:24). These are not easy words; in fact, as far as real life is concerned, they are the most difficult words in the entire Gospel. Our whole being, everything within us, rebels against these words.

Jesus, however, goes on to say, "For whoever wishes to save his life will lose it, but whoever loses his life for my sake will find it" (Mt 16:25). Let us stop for a moment and reflect on the words: "for my sake." Here we see the very essence of Jesus' claim, his self-awareness and the demands he makes of us. Jesus is at the heart of everything, he is the Son of God who is one with God the Father (cf. Jn 10:30), he is the one Savior (cf. Acts 4:12).

In effect, what seemed at first to be merely a stroke of bad luck or a tragedy not infrequently is shown to be a door which opens in our lives, leading to a greater good. But it is not always like this: many times, in this world, tragedies remain simply painful failures. Here again Jesus has something to tell us: after the Cross, he rose from the dead, and he rose as the firstborn among many brethren (cf. Rom 8:29; 1 Cor 15:20). His Cross can not be separated from his Resurrection. Only by believing in the Resurrection can we meaningfully advance along the Way of the Cross.

All:

Our Father . . .

Is there one who would not weep,
'Whelmed in miseries so deep,
Christ's dear Mother to behold?

13

SIXTH STATION

Veronica wipes the face of Jesus

V/. We adore you, O Christ, and we bless you.

R/. Because by your holy Cross you have redeemed the world.

From the Book of the Prophet Isaiah   53:2-3

There was in him no stately bearing to make us look at him,
nor appearance that would attract us to him.
He was spurned and avoided by men,
a man of suffering, accustomed to infirmity,
One of those from whom men hide their faces,
spurned, and we held him in no esteem.

MEDITATION

When Veronica wiped the face of Jesus with a cloth, that face must certainly not have been attractive; it was a disfigured face. And yet that face could not leave one indifferent; it was disturbing. It might provoke mockery and contempt, but also compassion, and even love, a desire to offer assistance. Veronica is the symbol of these emotions.

However disfigured, the face of Jesus nonetheless remains the face of the Son of God. It is a face marred by us, by the endless accumulation of human malice. But it is also a face marred for us, a face that expresses the loving sacrifice of Jesus and mirrors the infinite mercy of God the Father.

In the suffering face of Jesus we also see another accumulation: that of human suffering. And so Veronica's gesture of pity becomes a challenge to us, an urgent summons. It becomes a gentle but insistent demand not to turn away but to look with our own eyes at those who suffer, whether close at hand or far away. And not merely to look, but also to help. Tonight's Way of the Cross will not be fruitless if it leads us to practical acts of love and active solidarity.

All:

Our Father . . .

Can the human heart refrain
From partaking in her pain,
In that mother's pain untold?

JESUS FALLS THE SECOND TIME

V/. We adore you, O Christ, and we bless you.

R/. Because by your holy Cross you have redeemed the world.

From the Book of Psalms   41:6-10

My enemies say the worst of me:
    "When will that one die and be forgotten?"
When people come to visit me,
    they speak without sincerity.
Their hearts store up malice;
    they leave and spread their vicious lies.
My foes all whisper against me;
    they imagine the worst about me:
I have a deadly disease, they say;
    I will never rise from my sickbed.
Even the friend who had my trust,
    who shared my table, has scorned me.

MEDITATION

Once more Jesus falls beneath the Cross. He was, of course, physically
exhausted and mortally wounded at heart. He felt the burden of his

rejection by those who from the outset had obstinately opposed his mission. He felt the burden, in the end, of his rejection by the very people who seemed so full of admiration and even enthusiasm for him. Thus, gazing at the city which he loved so much, Jesus had cried out: "Jerusalem, Jerusalem . . . how many times I yearned to gather your children together, as a hen gathers her young under her wings, but you were unwilling!" (Mt 23:37). He felt the awful burden of his betrayal by Judas, his abandonment by the disciples at the hour of greatest trial; and in particular he felt the burden of his triple denial by Peter.

We know too that he was burdened down by the incalculable weight of our sins, the accumulation of offenses that down the centuries has accompanied the history of humanity.

And so, let us ask God, humbly yet confidently: Father, rich in mercy, help us not to add more weight to the Cross of Jesus. In the words of Pope John Paul II, who died five years ago tonight: "The limit imposed upon evil, of which man is both perpetrator and victim, is ultimately Divine Mercy" (*Memory and Identity*, p. 60).

All:

Our Father . . .

For the sins of his own nation
Saw him hang in desolation
Till his spirit forth he sent.

EIGHTH STATION

Jesus meets the women of Jerusalem who weep for him

V/. We adore you, O Christ, and we bless you.

R/. Because by your holy Cross you have redeemed the world.

From the Gospel according to Luke   23:27-29, 31

A large crowd of people followed Jesus, including many women who mourned and lamented him. Jesus turned to them and said, "Daughters of Jerusalem, do not weep for me; weep instead for yourselves and for your children, for indeed, the days are coming when people will say, 'Blessed are the barren, the wombs that never bore and the breasts that never nursed.'. . . For if these things are done when the wood is green what will happen when it is dry?"

MEDITATION

It is Jesus who takes pity on the women of Jerusalem, and on all of us. Even as he carries the Cross, Jesus remains the man who had compassion on the crowd (cf. Mk 8:2), who broke into tears before the tomb of Lazarus (cf. Jn 11:35), and who proclaimed blessed those who mourn, for they shall be comforted (cf. Mt 5:4).

In this way Jesus shows that he alone truly knows the heart of God the Father and can make it known to us: "No one knows the Father except the Son and anyone to whom the Son wishes to reveal him" (Mt 11:27).

From earliest times humanity has asked, often with anguish, how God relates to us. Is it with providential care, sovereign indifference, or even disdain and hatred? No certain answer can be given to this kind of question if we merely rely on the resources of our understanding, our experience, or even our heart.

That is why Jesus—in his life and his teaching, his Cross and his Resurrection—is by far the greatest event in all human history, the light that illumines our destiny.

All:

Our Father . . .

O sweet Mother! font of love,
Touch my spirit from above,
Make my heart with yours accord.

NINTH STATION

Jesus falls the third time

V/. We adore you, O Christ, and we bless you.

R/. Because by your holy Cross you have redeemed the world.

From the second Letter of Saint Paul to the Corinthians   5:19-21

God was reconciling the world to himself in Christ, not counting their trespasses against them and entrusting to us the message of reconciliation. . . . We implore you on behalf of Christ, be reconciled to God. For our sake he made him to be sin who did not know sin, so that we might become the righteousness of God in him.

MEDITATION

The real reason why Christ fell repeatedly was not simply his physical sufferings or human betrayal, but the will of the Father. That mysterious will, humanly incomprehensible, yet infinitely good and generous, whereby Jesus became "sin for us." All the sins of humanity were placed upon him, and that mysterious exchange took place whereby we sinners became "the righteousness of God."

In our efforts to identify ourselves completely with Jesus as he walks and falls beneath the Cross, it is right for us to have feelings of repentance and sorrow. But stronger still should be the feeling of gratitude welling up in our hearts.

Yes, Lord, you have redeemed us, you have set us free; by your Cross you have made us righteous before God. You have also joined us so deeply to yourself that we too have been made, in you, God's children, members of his household and his friends. Thank you Lord; may gratitude toward you be the distinguishing mark of our lives.

All:

Our Father ...

Make me feel as you have felt;
Make my soul to glow and melt
With the love of Christ, my Lord.

Jesus is stripped of his garments

V/. We adore you, O Christ, and we bless you.

R/. Because by your holy Cross you have redeemed the world.

From the Gospel according to John   19: 23-24

[The soldiers] took his clothes and divided them into four shares, a share for each soldier. They also took his tunic, but the tunic was seamless, woven in one piece from the top down. So they said to one another, "Let's not tear it, but cast lots for it to see whose it will be," in order that the passage of scripture might be fulfilled [that says]:

> *"They divided my garments among them,
>   and for my vesture they cast lots."*

MEDITATION

Jesus is stripped of his garments. We have reached the final act of the tragedy, begun with the arrest in the Garden of Olives, in which Jesus is stripped of his dignity as a human being, much less than as God's Son.

Jesus appears naked before the eyes of the inhabitants of Jerusalem and the eyes of all humanity. In a profound way it is right that this should be so. For he divested his very self in order to sacrifice himself for our sake. So the gesture of being stripped of his garments is also the fulfillment of a prophecy of Holy Scripture.

As we look upon Jesus naked on the Cross, we feel deep within us a compelling need to look upon our own nakedness, to stand spiritually naked before ourselves, but first of all before God and before our brothers and sisters in humanity. We need to be stripped of the pretence of appearing better than we are, and to seek to be sincere and transparent.

The way of acting that, perhaps more than any other, provoked Jesus' disdain was hypocrisy. How often did he tell his disciples not to act "as the hypocrites do" (Mt 6:2, 5, 16). Or say to those who impugned his good deeds: "Woe to you, hypocrites" (Mt 23:13, 15, 23, 25, 27, 29).

Lord Jesus, hanging naked on the Cross, grant that I too may stand naked before you.

All:

Our Father . . .

Holy Mother, pierce me through,
In my heart each wound renew
Of my Savior crucified.

Jesus is nailed to the Cross

V/. We adore you, O Christ, and we bless you.

R/. Because by your holy Cross you have redeemed the world.

From the Gospel according to Mark   15:25-27

It was nine o'clock in the morning when they crucified him. The inscription of the charge against him read, "The King of the Jews." With him they crucified two revolutionaries, one on his right and one on his left.

Meditation

Jesus is nailed to the Cross. An appalling form of torture. And as he hangs on the Cross, many of the passersby mock him and even try to provoke him: "He saved others; he cannot save himself. . . . He trusted in God; let him deliver him now if he wants him. For he said: 'I am the Son of God'" (Mt 27:42-43). Not only is his person mocked, but also his saving mission, the mission that Jesus was bringing to fulfillment upon the Cross.

Yet deep within, Jesus knows an incomparably greater suffering, which causes him to cry out, "My God, my God, why have you forsaken me?" (Mk 15:34). These are the opening words of a Psalm which concludes with a reaffirmation of complete trust in God. At the same time they are words to be taken completely seriously, as expressing the greatest test to which Jesus was subjected.

How many times, when we are tested, we think that we have been forgotten or abandoned by God. Or are even tempted to decide that God does not exist.

The Son of God, who drank his bitter chalice to the dregs and then rose from the dead, tells us, instead, with his whole self, by his life and by his death, that we ought to trust in God. We can believe him.

All:

Our Father . . .

Let me share with you his pain,
Who for all our sins was slain,
Who for me in torments died.

Jesus dies on the Cross

V/. We adore you, O Christ, and we bless you.

R/. Because by your holy Cross you have redeemed the world.

From the Gospel according to John   19:28-30

*After this, aware that everything was now finished, in order that the scrip-
ture might be fulfilled, Jesus said, "I thirst." There was a vessel filled with
common wine. So they put a sponge soaked in wine on a sprig of hyssop
and put it up to his mouth. When Jesus had taken the wine, he said, "It is
finished." And bowing his head, he handed over the spirit.*

Meditation

Whenever death comes after a painful illness, it is customary to say
with some relief, "He is no longer suffering." In a certain sense, these
words also apply to Jesus. Yet these words are all too limited and super-
ficial in the face of any person's death, and even more so in the face of
the Death of that man who is the Son of God.

When Jesus dies, the veil of the Temple of Jerusalem is torn in two
and other signs occur, causing the Roman centurion to exclaim as he

stands guard beneath the Cross, "Truly, this was the Son of God!" (cf. Mt 27:51-54).

In truth, nothing is as dark and mysterious as the Death of the Son of God, who with God the Father is the source and fullness of life. Yet at the same time, nothing shines so brightly, for here the glory of God shines forth, the glory of all-powerful and merciful Love.

In the face of Jesus' Death, our response is the silence of adoration. In this way we entrust ourselves to him, we place ourselves in his hands, and we beg him that nothing, in our life or in our death, may ever separate us from him (cf. Rom 8:38-39).

All:

Our Father . . .

For the sins of his own nation
Saw him hang in desolation
Till his spirit forth he sent.

Jesus is taken down from the Cross and placed in the arms of his Mother

V/. We adore you, O Christ, and we bless you.

R/. Because by your holy Cross you have redeemed the world.

From the Gospel according to John   2:1-5

There was a wedding in Cana in Galilee, and the mother of Jesus was there. Jesus and his disciples were also invited to the wedding. When the wine ran short, the mother of Jesus said to him, "They have no wine." [And] Jesus said to her, "Woman, how does your concern affect me? My hour has not yet come." His mother said to the servers, "Do whatever he tells you."

MEDITATION

Now the hour of Jesus has been completed and Jesus is taken down from the Cross. Ready to receive him are the arms of his Mother. After having tasted the loneliness of death to the bitter end, Jesus immediately rediscovers—in his lifeless body—the strongest and sweetest of his human bonds, the warmth of his Mother's affection. The greatest artists—we need but think for example of Michelangelo's *Pietà*—have been able to intuit and express the depth and indestructible strength of this bond.

As we remember that Mary, standing at the foot of the Cross, also became the mother of each one of us, we ask her to put into our hearts the feelings that unite her to Jesus. To be authentic Christians, to follow Jesus truly, we need to be bound to him with all that is within us: our minds, our will, our hearts, our daily choices great and small.

Only in this way can God stand at the center of our lives. Only in this way can he be something more than a source of consolation which is ever close when needed, but without interfering with the concrete interests governing our daily lives and decisions.

All:

Our Father . . .

Let me mingle tears with you,
Mourning him who mourned for me,
All the days that I may live.

Jesus is placed in the tomb

V/. We adore you, O Christ, and we bless you.

R/. Because by your holy Cross you have redeemed the world.

From the Gospel according to Matthew   27:57-60

When it was evening, there came a rich man from Arimathea named Joseph, who was himself a disciple of Jesus. He went to Pilate and asked for the body of Jesus; then Pilate ordered it to be handed over. Taking the body, Joseph wrapped it [in] clean linen and laid it in his new tomb that he had hewn in the rock. Then he rolled a huge stone across the entrance to the tomb and departed.

MEDITATION

With the stone that seals the entrance to the tomb, it all appears to be over. Yet could the Author of life remain a prisoner of death? This is why the tomb of Jesus, from that time forward, has not only been the object of the most intense devotion, but has also provoked the deepest divisions of minds and hearts. Herein lies the parting of the ways between those who believe in Christ and those who do not, even if many of them consider him an extraordinary man.

Soon that tomb would remain empty, and it has never been possible to find a convincing explanation for the fact of its being empty other than the one given by the witnesses to Jesus' Resurrection from the dead, from Mary Magdalene to Peter and the other Apostles.

Let us halt in prayer before the tomb of Jesus, asking God for the eyes of faith so that we too can become witnesses of his Resurrection. Thus may the Way of the Cross become for us too a wellspring of life.

All:

Our Father . . .

While my body here decays,
May my soul your goodness praise,
Safe in heaven eternally.

Amen.

ADDRESS OF THE HOLY FATHER AND APOSTOLIC BLESSING

The Holy Father addresses those present.

At the end of his address, the Holy Father imparts the Apostolic Blessing:

V/. The Lord be with you.

R/. And also with you.

V/. Blessed be the name of the Lord.

R/. Now and for ever.

V/. Our help is in the name of the Lord.

R/. Who made heaven and earth.

V/. May almighty God bless you, the Father, and the Son, and the Holy Spirit.

R/. Amen.

ADDRESS OF HIS HOLINESS
BENEDICT XVI

PALATINE HILL

Dear Brothers and Sisters,

This evening, in stillness and moved in heart, we have journeyed in prayer along the Way of the Cross. We have gone up Calvary with Jesus, and we have meditated on his suffering, rediscovering how deep his love was and is for us. But let us not limit ourselves to a compassion dictated be weak sentiment; rather, we wish to participate in the sufferings of Jesus, we wish to accompany our Master, to share his Passion in our lives, in the life of the Church, for the life of the world, since we know that it is precisely in the Lord's Cross, in love without limits, that he gives everything of himself, is the source of grace, of liberation, of peace, of salvation.

The texts, the meditations, and the prayers of the *Way of the Cross* have helped us to consider the mystery of the Passion in order to appreciate the great lesson of love which God gave on the Cross, that there might be born in us a renewed desire to change our hearts, living each day that love which is the only force able to change the world.

This evening we have gazed upon Jesus and his countenance marked by pain, derided, outraged, and disfigured by the sin of humanity; tomorrow night we will look upon the same countenance full of joy, radiant and luminous. From the moment Jesus goes into the tomb, the tomb and death are no longer a place without hope where history stops in the most complete failure, where man touches the extreme limit of his powerlessness. Good Friday is the greatest day of hope, come to fruition upon the Cross, as Jesus dies, as he draws his last breath, crying out with a loud voice, "Father, into your hands I commend my spirit" (Lk 23:46). Entrusting his "given" existence into the Father's hands, he knows that his Death is becoming the source of life, just as the seed in the earth must be destroyed that a new plant may be born: "If a grain of wheat falls into the earth and dies, it remains alone; but if it dies, it bears much fruit" (Jn 12:24). Jesus is the grain of wheat that falls to the earth, is split open, is destroyed and dies, and for this very reason is able to bear fruit. From the day on which Christ was raised upon it, the Cross, which had seemed to be a sign of desolation, of abandonment, and of failure, has become a new beginning: from the profundity of death is raised the promise of eternal life. The victorious splendor of the dawning day of Easter already shines upon the Cross.

In the silence of this night, in the silence which envelops Holy Saturday, touched by the limitless love of God, we live in the hope of the dawn of the third day, the dawn of the victory of God's love, the luminous daybreak which allows the eyes of our heart to see afresh our life, its difficulties, its suffering. Our failures, our disappointments, our bitterness, which seem to signal that all is lost, are instead illumined by hope. The act of love upon the Cross is confirmed by the Father, and the dazzling light of the Resurrection enfolds and transforms everything: friendship can be born from betrayal, pardon from denial, love from hate.

Grant us, Lord, to carry our cross with love, and to carry our daily crosses in the certainty that they have been enlightened by the dazzling light of Easter. Amen.

OTHER TITLES

Pope Benedict XVI offers inspiration and encouragement through this collection of titles in the Spiritual Thoughts Series:

The Eucharist
No. 7-084, 120 pp.

Family
No. 7-075, 107 pp.

Following Christ
No. 7-056, 132 pp.

Mary
No. 7-054, 172 pp.

The Priesthood
No. 7-086, 96 pp.

The Saints
No. 7-055, 164 pp.

St. Paul
No. 7-053, 128 pp.

Sickness
No. 7-137, 78 pp.

The Word of God
No. 7-065, 100 pp.

Pope Benedict XVI
Spiritual Thoughts:
In the First Year of
His Papacy
No. 5-765, 128 pp.

To order these resources or to obtain a catalog of other USCCB titles, visit *www.usccbpublishing.org* or call toll-free 800-235-8722. In the Washington metropolitan area or from outside the United States, call 202-722-8716. Para pedidos en español, llame al 800-235-8722 y presione 4 para hablar con un representante del servicio al cliente en español.